Paper Tiger

Written and illustrated by Nicola Senior

Collins

Minmin's home was a flat at the top of his grandad's diner.

Minmin was sorting the fortune cookies for that evening. Grandad was cutting peppers and carrots into little shapes on a plate.

There was a lot to chop and scrape, so Grandad told Minmin a tale about a wild tiger to keep their spirits up.

Grandad explained that in China, people used to think that tigers can get rid of a thief or even put out a fire.

Minmin woke up the next day and saw a proud tiger crouching on his bedside dresser.

Grandad had made it by folding paper.

It had been folded to look like it was leaping across streams and lakes in the wild.

"I think my teacher will like it," said Minmin.

"Wow, that's so cool," said Naz.
Jamie didn't think it was cool at all.
Jamie grabbed the tiger from Minmin.

He pounded it flat with his fist.

"You have spoilt it!" Minmin shouted. He ran out of the room bursting with anger.

At home, Grandad helped Minmin understand that Jamie had made a mistake.

"I think Jamie would like a tiger himself," said Grandad.

Grandad made a bold tiger for Minmin.

He made a paper tiger for Jamie too.

Grandad was wise and told Minmin to be kind.

Jamie was in the cloakroom, feeling full of shame.

It was hard for Minmin to offer the tiger to Jamie, but he was brave.

Jamie admitted his mistake and both boys gave a wide smile.

They shook hands and played a game of tigers, chasing crocodiles, behind the maze of trees.

Minmin's feelings

 Review: After reading

Use your assessment from hearing the children read to choose any GPCs, words or tricky words that need additional practice.

Read 1: Decoding
- Check the children's understanding of the following words by looking at them in context and suggesting synonyms.
    - page 4 – **spirits**: talk about the whole phrase **keep their spirits up** and how it means to "stay cheerful"
    - page 11 – **pounded**: talk about how **pounded** is different to "hit", in that it is a repeated action that flattens the tiger
- Ask the children to look for words containing the /igh/ sound. Ask them to point to the letter or letters that make the sound. Repeat for the /ai/ sound.
- Point to words and encourage the children to read each word, blending the word in their heads before saying it aloud. How quickly can they read the word fluently?

Read 2: Prosody
- Turn to page 12, and ask the children why there's an exclamation mark after Minmin's spoken words. (*to show that he's upset and shouting*)
- Ask children to read Minmin's words with expression.
- Look at page 13 together and discuss the reason for the comma. Ask: Which bit of the sentence is it separating? (*the part that tells us that Minmin is now at home*)
- Ask children to read page 13, pausing at the comma, and then read it again without pausing. Ask: Which reading sounds better?

Read 3: Comprehension
- Ask the children if they have ever taken something to school to show everyone. Ask them to describe it, and why it was important to them.
- Discuss what Minmin had to do to be kind. (*give a tiger to Jamie*) Ask: Was it easy or hard for Minmin? (*hard, because Jamie had destroyed his tiger*) Broaden the discussion out into the children's own experiences of being kind.
- Explore the characters' thoughts and feelings through role play.
    - Encourage a child to role play Jamie on page 10, and suggest how they feel.
    - Ask a child to role play Minmin on page 19, and say how they feel about Jamie, and why.
    - Repeat for page 20. How does each boy feel and why?
- Turn to pages 22–23 and ask the children to talk through Minmin's feelings at different points of the story, using the pictures as prompts.